PAGAN

PAGAN

Poems by John Corley

Cover Art by Carly Thaw
Cover Design by Casey Chiappetta
Text Design by Sonia Tabriz

Edited by Susan Nagelsen & Charles Huckelbury

BleakHouse Publishing
2018

BleakHouse Publishing

Ward Circle Building 254
American University
Washington, DC 20016

NEC Box 67
New England College
Henniker, New Hampshire 03242

www.BleakHousePublishing.com

Robert Johnson – Editor & Publisher
Sonia Tabriz - Managing Editor
Liz Calka - Creative Director
Casey Chiappetta – Chief Operating Officer
Alyssa Purdy – Chief Editorial Officer
Emily Dalgo – Chief Development Officer
Rachel Ternes – Chief Creative Officer
Jacob Bray – Art Director

ISBN-13: 978-0-9961162-4-4

Printed in the United States of America

For Georgia Anne

Table of Contents

Acknowledgments

Everlasting gratitude to my mother, who gave me her creativity, and my father, who gave me his grit. Robert Johnson, Susan Nagelsen, Charles Huckelbury, and the editorial and creative staff at BleakHouse Publishing have been indescribably dedicated and supportive. A special thank you to Marianne Fisher-Giorlando, Ph.D., whose inspiration and encouragement is largely responsible for this volume.

Introduction

Drawing on his personal experiences and an uncanny ability to describe the indescribable, John Corley guides the reader on a walking tour of the light and dark sides of the street, accompanied by a demonstrated intimacy with both. His work is not for the faint hearted, but an understated compassion moderates, for example, his treatment of personal and institutional violence. By drawing back the curtain on the intrinsic human capacity for predation, he concomitantly allows us to contemplate the possibility of change and juxtaposes that possibility with a restrained optimism. An expressed longing for an earlier time, when society was governed more by respect for human value than the current political avarice that garners current headlines, keeps his work grounded in the present and will have heads nodding in agreement. John Corley is a poet of immense power and range. His work speaks at once to the heart and the head, pulling us inexorably into his world, a world that would be foreign to us but for his profound humanism and direct, often searing language. With great skill, Corley uses the fine art of poetry to guide us on a compelling tour that often touches on the underside of life in and out of prison. Corley's creations sparkle with heat and insight, lighting the way through regions dark and dangerous, enticing and forbidding, and then deliver us, edified and enriched, to a world of hard-won hope.

Susan Nagelsen & Charles Huckelbury, Editors
Robert Johnson, Publisher

PART I

By way of introduction

I suppose you wonder
who I am
           author of this poor verse.
You don't know me.
You won't

           ever

know me.

I'm detached from your dignitarial parades.
Cheers and salutes to the comfortably acceptable
do not apply to me
yet.

I'm the banished boy
           (Oh, you remember)
cast out any number of years ago
           (They're all the same, the years: forever).
Fell off my mountain one summer,
fell intellect deep into swamp muck,
blew a bubble that fought its way
through slime to stolen sunshine and
exploded with a proclamation of counter-contempt.

Don't try to feel for me.
You can't.

I am the whispers of gathered secrets.
I am the storm in stormless skies.
I am the pie in the face of a holy
           cud-chewing society.
I am blood and depth that demand a hearing.

I am
           a
poet.   That's all you need to know.

1 a.m. in Ash-3

In winter, sleeping
convicts shrouded in tattered

state-issue blankets head
to toe are corpses stiff in the tomb
where we live, 86
dead men waiting to die

and make it official. Their corpses
snore and fart and hack
all night, their sounds and smells
telltale proof of ghosts,

endless haunting —when one
specter passes to the light another
takes his place,
like a shark's teeth, death

lined up and waiting. The dorm
at night is a refugee camp,
shower-washed apparel
draped over bed rails to dry,

whites and shirts better
preserved than the laundry's indifferent
treatment can offer—rags
or flags stirred by industrial

heaters clinging to a never
cleaned ceiling, once white
now webbed,
the little brown spiders

who live up there prone
to descend to the snorers below for
a sampling of blood. How
can so many so

soundly sleep, blanketed,
as those damned heaters blow
their sinuses dry?
Mechanisms temperature-controlled

but the old zombies, perpetually

cold sacks of bones, stack ice
cups on the housing
to trick the system. I curse

and take the cups away.
The place reeks of men crammed
together. Toilets
leak, sinks drip,

shower water seeps
beneath the cracked splash-guard
and puddles in the corner.
I shower because I have to,

aware of the filth around me,
used-up soap slivers, strewn wrappers,
hair and the tiny
moisture-worshiping worms

that burrow through the caulking.
Even in winter someone's
always on the crapper.
They flush and the smell climbs

up the shower drain.
I catch my breath and take my
time; the water (God
knows what grows in the ancient

pipes) is hot, and I like
the water better than the heaters.
My bed's
a thin cotton-stuffed sheath,

flat in the middle where I've slept
for six years. New ones are hard
to come by.
The budget, right? I dissected

a mattress once and pulled
out its guts, stuffed the stale
cotton into a cheap tote
bag some charitable Christian

group distributed at Christmas
to make my pillow. It's softer than
the state's neck-breaker.
My sheets are self-bleached.

Flat green blanket courtesy,
U.S. Army, when swarms of
Katrina-displaced prisoners
were dumped on Angola in '05.

I got mine from a guy
named Joe who went home,
one of the lucky ones.
Maybe his ex-blanket's

lucky. I rarely use
it in winter, thanks to the heaters, but
in summer, under the fan,
I hide in darkness and dreams.

Summer finds men in white
boxers haphazard across their
racks, vying for the slightest
breeze from the big fans

strategically stationed front
and back of the three double-bunked
rows for maximum
cooling. Mine is the worst

bunk in the house, up front,
a heavy-traffic area,
loud (I never sleep
without ear plugs),

dirty, shit-smelling crappers
nearby, but the fan for the middle
row is right there,
mine, except for the hottest

nights keeping me hunkered
beneath my green blanket while
most others sweat,
curse, and wish they had

my bunk. Stifling nights
inspire the zombies too;
the dorm never completely
rests in summer. Men

shuffle all hours
back and forth, to the crappers, to

6

the TV room fans, to anywhere
a breeze offers relief.

Middle-aisle guys who can't
Afford to pay to rig a fan
aimed their way
suffer. It's the unfair, unchanging

way of the jungle. Sleep
arrives stubbornly. I read until
I can't remember
the words I just read.

History is my favorite
but omissions piss me off: the
crucial moments, the trek
to the siege, the assassin's motivations,

discoveries in the blackened ruins
of ancient citadels. The old men snore and
I read, maybe
literature instead to speed

the process along; sometimes
I crave my dreams and the freedom
from prison they bring. Sometimes
I wouldn't mind if I never

woke again. Sleep
is escape. Death is liberation.

The marvelous manly men of old

In the magical misty days of old,
when wizened men were strong and bold,
lived by sword and legends told
of thunder, fire, gleaming gold,
for honor, god, inherent right,
shepherd, merchant, chain-mailed knight
were for their peace compelled to fight
when devils came by cloak of night,
or rallied on blinding battlefields;
men of old refused to yield,
raised their blades and battle shields
to meet the challenge unconcealed
without the faintest fleck of fear,
without a single doubt or tear,
with purpose but to persevere,
eradicate the lustful leer
of enemy charging across the green
(a spirit now we've rarely seen).

Proud and brave with bodies lean,
honed by hardship, matchless keen
to protect the tiny parceled place
they called their own, the private space
worth the risk of death's embrace,
and if with death a man was faced
he faced it with his head held high,
gave no ground when doom drew nigh,
stared it in its moldy eye,
fought to failure, defeat defy.

Ah, for those long lost lordly days
of simpler pace, simpler ways
when men would not their values raze
for coin, cowardice, love of praise,
but strict obeyed an ancient plan,
a hard day's work with calloused hands,
unafraid to take a stand.

And stand they did, with strength of pride
than rather from misfortune hide,
they warred against oppressing tides
and thus, they lived and bravely died
for things in which they firm believed
with passions only death relieved.

These were men, champions free,
laughing when the enemy
presumed to overrun the good
of values born where good men stood.
Men themselves were solid then,
noblest there have ever been,
knowing when to war and when
a helping hand to others lend.
Such were times of chivalry,
forgotten from antiquity:
a man displayed obstinacy
when challenge forced audacity.

Ancient seas, kingdoms far,
journeys traveled by North Star;
the men of old a curious breed,
an endless world to wonder feed–
      "The parcel here is mine to claim
      but out beyond the distant plain
      amazements I must run to see
      and thus fulfill my destiny."
So off they went if go alone
they must into the vast unknown,
from England's chalky white-faced banks
to Gaul's resplendent purple ranks,
throughout the wildish land of Huns,
past the Adriatic's sons
to Buda-Pest, Marmora,
Nordic ice, Ankara;
they crossed the Volga, swam the Nile,
sailed onto the Persian isles,
weighed the markets of Ceylon,
traipsed the halls of Babylon,

dared the untamed lands beyond
(a lesson here to understand,
the key to what completes the man:
a man is restless in his soul,
his human nature unconsoled
to idly dwell in peace before
in peace the awesome world explore).
The call of men in younger years,
adventure molds one' s latter years.
Experience tempers civility,
knowledge sates curiosity.
To travel wide bears strong commend
to wanderlust and tension spend.
Diverse cultures, strange, hypnotic;

distant cities, distant wines,
clustered jungles, diamond mines—
young man, go into the world,
into the melee willing hurl
your youthful questions; into the fold
immerse yourself like men of old.
A man can only testify
to what he's seen with his own eye,
by nature hungry for all things,
what man is calm when each day brings
another span of nothing known
of mystic lands beyond his home?
Little wonder now we've grown
bored with daily routine cares;
we've never ventured anywhere.

But men of old, those wondrous men,
for destiny rode into the wind
in search of what lay there to find,
thus achieved a peace of mind
elusive in these modern days
when so-called men prefer to laze
in comfortable arms of technology,
spill their worries in therapy,
in peril's wake to run and hide
and contemplate their suicide
when storm clouds cast away the sun;
the weary race is left unwon
by men who claim they've earned the right
to be called men, consumed by fright.

Review, my son, what you have learned
of ancient ways now sorely spurned.
Compare what made a man back then
with how our world defines its men:
they were solid, rugged, proud and bold,
adventurers, conquerors, kings of old;
god, family, land they prized,
life's hardships made them early wise.
They were loyal, true, lived for cause,
lived according to nature's laws.
They fought when honor was at stake,
for honor they would not forsake.
That's the way it was back then
in younger times when men were men.

Times have changed, become complex;
men no longer muscles flex

but passive watch the world go by,
surrender freely all the pie
for fear that someone's precious rights
should one assert his manly might,
will be perverted in our courts,
recorded in adverse reports
for all the damning world to read;
man has lost his noble creed.
Today's politically correct
forbids you dare to resurrect
chivalric values for yourself
lest you lose to someone else
who doesn't deserve the time of day,
refuses to work to earn his way,
fills his hands with all he owns
with charity the state condones,
lest you wear society's brand,
biased, racist, fascist man,
rebellious, antisocial man:
a game so sad, a lifetime spent
means nothing to the government,
corrupt, untrue, full of greed,
without a care for people's needs.
Except for lessers they embrace,
laggards of the human race
lifted up and glorified,
given history, given pride,
with nothing ever being earned.
What a sickly course we've turned,
how they fiddle while we burn
in stupidity, hail the god equality,
the least of things that men can be.
Men are satisfied to know
the truth as liars tell them so;
flabby bodies, flabby minds,
searching at their feet to find
fulfillment they will never know.
They buried fulfillment long ago.

But don't despair the manly wake;
the one thing fools can't ever take
is what we are inside,
inherent code we thought had died
but dormant waits the strength of will.
The man of old lives proudly still
within the deepest, truest part
of each man's spirit, each man's heart.
It's up to each to take a stand

against society's brainwashed man.
Listen to the voice within
that rightly guides the course of men;
a sword does not a true man make,
nor violence for pleasure's sake.
The warrior's basic code and creed
is never follow paths of greed,
respect all things in daily life,
do not seek to take a wife
until you feel you've done and seen
the world that offers everything
(until the world has sated you
to no one dear will you be true).
Nourish pride in all you own,
reap the harvest you have sown.
Let no lesser man invade
the private circle you have laid.
Hold a faith in something pure,
never run from meeting your
debts to god, self, family.
Don't exploit the frailty
of any tiny living thing:
such arrogance with it downfall brings.

And lift a toast to men of old,
those stately warriors wise and bold
who lived according to their souls.
We today should reach inside,
awaken our remissive pride.
We should show the world we can
live each one a doubtless man,
wise and noble, peaceful man
commanding respect of friend and foe
like real men did back long ago.

Before she sleeps

Before she sleeps
the young, blonde wife
thirsting for truth
drinks all alone
with no fear of the night.

Kiss

It's a talent acquired, perfected, an art, a kiss;
tactfully approached with coy affection
and quickened heart.

It's surrender, conquest, a pulsing, rushing heart
that fires the secret, sleeping imaginings
of the soul in a moment's quiet fury.

Rhythmic, a waltz to a lovers' song it is,
a giving, taking, leading, following,
a talent acquired, perfected, an art, a kiss.

Secret glances

Secret glances
happenstance dances
interest sparked
potential remarked
private meeting
time is fleeting
forbidden fruit
vows taboo
lightning pleasure
devil's treasure
free to choose
bound to lose
free to lie
apt to die.

Spins

A wheel spins in a pallid wind, broken
by time-bent bulrushes wafting along creosote
perimeters. One size fits all.

A wheel, misshapen, tarnished, whining in oblong
agony, anemic gatekeeper guarding idealized
yesterdays. Where is everyone?

It's never the same,
the place from where we came.

Shadows arm in arm pirouette, parapet's
edge, jagged scenes and mezzanines,
ghostly lost obsessions from nether regions.

Who told Dana not to tell Mom,
or Donna Sue not to even think it?
Bad things happen in the closet. It burns.

The multiverse pulls, pulses, picks
and chooses winners, losers, echoes blossom
across dimensions: can't go back. It's done.

Dreams are sweet, sure, sure, but shit.
I wish I could have saved her. I tried. She died.

Every thought, every choice, every
flicker flicked from the fire forces forgotten
faces against the wall, blindfolded and cigarette

balanced on razor spines, above the trench.
Dina and Tina died young, prisoners
now to uninhibited unimaginables.

A wheel spins in the dark, monotone cry
peeling what's left of the paint from Camelot.
Can't change it, can't recall the whistle's shrill
announcement. Banality flows south.
Picture-perfect portrait, the clapboard cabin
wavering in the cold sun, a brisk reminder

what's done is done.

Sleep, Jessie

For Jessica Lunsford, whose life was stolen in the night by John Evander Couey, February 2005

They found her
in a double trash bag casket
knotted at the head and feet
covered with leaves
less than two football fields
from her bed
where she slept when
the devil came calling
from the Homosassee night,
through the window
while her parents dreamed.

It was poor,
this Florida home but
it held love—
her rail-thin daddy with his
missing teeth and worker's cap
cried in the cameras three weeks
when he wasn't searching,
woods walking,
begging "Jessie! Jessie!"
hoping—

We all saw her smile on TV, and
we loved her too, and
we hoped too,
although these things rarely end well.
And the days passed.

He'd done it before,
preyed on innocence, the
defenseless ones,
got a little slap
did a little time
a little time
too little time;
this time he took more.
This time he took her,
bound and buried her alive,
kneeling, clutching
a purple stuffed dolphin,

and this is how she died.
She was only nine.

They found her
twenty-three days later
in a double trash bag casket
knotted at the head and feet
covered with leaves
a glance from her own bed.

Sleep soft my sweet, sleep
sound at peace
until your soul returns.
Most of us didn't know you but
we felt your touch, the
gift that woke us up
and somehow made us better
for caring,
made us rally against the devils,
made us aware too late
for you but because of you
in time to save others.

*Previously published in *Exiled Voices, Portals of Discovery* (Nagelsen, 2008)

The river

I sat and smoked and wondered what
to do with my next moment.
My mind left and kept going,
drifting on a river of time.

Drifting calmly, floating by
memories long forgotten.
I smile at scenes that once made me cry,
complacent in the river.

There on the shore, when I was a child–
moment frozen like wax images–
drifting past days I was wild,
days which hold no meaning.

Young and old, now and then,
what do these mean?
Can't return to yesterday
when I lived beside the river.

I see them all, staring across the river
with empty eyes and sad faces.
They can't see me
as I float into quiet places.

I leave it all, hopes, dreams, plans,
on the river's dirty shore,
sever my sinful hands.
There's no pain in the river.

Float, float, drift along the river,
back to my beginnings;
the water's warmth calms my shivers.
Farewell to ghosts.

When I reach the river's end
I'll reach to take the offered hand
and discover at last what it's all about
as I wait along the river.

December

December found us stooped and sweating
in a ditch in an Angola field
while Grandmother lay sprouting tubes
a million miles away in a hospital bed.

All the sons and daughters
bleary-eyed and weary
stood around and thought
my god how old we've gotten.
The sun bleached my hair.

On the Texas side of Toledo Bend

By the lake—she, topless on the sand
china doll, white as mare's milk, beautiful—
She loved him then,
and they were united against
the troublesome,
confusing, unfair world.

They were together
and young.

He oiled her skin
with his calloused hands,
deliberate, over her flat belly.
Her slender legs were so warm,
she was pale
and soft in the sun.

She grinned and looked for voyeurs
as he oiled her breasts,
their gentle roundness,
piercing excitement,

her blue eyes more dazzling
than any lake or sea, sky or gem,
and he loved her more than he ever had.

That day, unforgotten
as long as he lives,
they made a child,
conceived of pure relentless
love between two hearts.

Obstinate

It's the rebel in me.

I won't allow them the pleasure of whispering he's
cracking—
I'll do it quietly, privately, totally and no one
will suspect until it's too late to paste me back together.
I won't invite them to the good night's rage,
where I morph into an inky black vacuum.

Just sweep up the slivers and go about your business.

It's a dilemma because
I don't know how to give up. I've never done it before.
I wasn't taught to yield to adversity but stand my ground,
stand and resist when weaker ones haven't the strength—
I've stood so long I'm rooted alone above
a battlefield strewn with my lost life's debris—
is it really me?

I don't recognize myself.

I've changed so. Grown old. Grown cold.
I don't know how to give up. Maybe I'm someone else
now, mimicking someone who faded away
who didn't know how to give up and it just
doesn't matter what I do— no one will know
and we'll all fade away too soon enough.

Slim

The last of the old breed, the dying dinosaur–
bad liver, bad back, left
eye dull and blind, bone thin, tall
as an undertaker, inked from one
end to the other— White Power, dagger,
swastika, R.I.P., bare breasted barfly whose boobs
loll slightly off-kilter— still combing gray hair too sparse
to comb: one crazy mother, high
when he can be, pissed when he can't, the implausible
terminus untamed after 40 in and proud of it.

I buy my moods from Slim. Garbage highs,
generic anti-seizure and relaxers, nothing
to brag about but they soften my mood, and I need
that. The scores make me sociable,

help me laugh, a buck
apiece, payable in canteen or contraband
smokes. They don't show up in the cup.

Eight beans for breakfast and the day flows:
I wake in the wee hours, breathless, counting
down to my next handful of oblong peace.

Slim's the orderly. He sways glassy-eyed
in a nonexistent breeze in the middle of the dorm,
death grip on his broom handle, loaded to the gills.
His life is jails and prisons,
a juvenile offender, escape artist, repeat
fuckup. He has no tales that aren't crime–

rooted, no life beyond wasting life,
but it's his life, and who else can judge
(except the judge)? He schemes to go home
but secretly, I think, he knows he's already there,
and the people of the world will never let him out.
He cut a man's throat. Says he didn't. But he did.

Slim whispers his plot to revolt against
Angola's high indignity, legislative
indifference; force in the feds to shake this mutha
up. He'll slice his arms. His friends will slice theirs.
In rush the media; it's a huge scandal, what
the hell is going on in Angola? He won't

work, his friends won't work, they'll shut
the place down, and the people will beg them to please
tell us what's wrong. That's the out, Slim says.

Things will change, Slim says. Except,
they won't. Give him 10 minutes, and the plot
is forgotten. He sways on his broom handle, the last
dinosaur, waiting for the cataclysmic end.

Toro Bottom

Fifteen pills for breakfast—two brown, three
orange, four white, six yellow sunny
side up, please—and I lost Monday.

Breathless woke, unable to decode
the clock hands. The day passed in a puff,
ingloriously neglected. I vowed to do better
on Tuesday, so I skipped an orange, flopped
down and framed dissected memories through a lucid
sliver. Somewhere a whistle blew. I shook

my head, cursed the universe, and dreamed my dreams.

Out at Plainview, a potholed asphalt afterthought,
looping through the boonies west of Florien, the wild woods
turn docile when winter drives the less-dressed chatterers
into community huddles in dark burrows against the cold.

Still, sweatered cat and fox squirrels
romp on bony branches in the canopy above
the frosted carpeting surrendered by seasonal greenery.
A white-tail might tiptoe along the narrow
light-speckled trails tamped by armadillo paws
and the heavy hooves of the occasional boar descended
from domestic escapees during great-grandpa's day.

The trails are a spidery maze that may lead to
the forks of Mill and Toro creeks or to
a thicket so thick it's a prison to novice venturers.

Plain-clothed wood ducks seasonally excited
paddle their little orange paddlers ninety
to nothing in the caramel creek where the banks bend
at random angles and the water runs thick and sluggish
and the squirrels play above the ducks that pay
no attention, dispelling the myth that ducks fear all
sound and movement not their own and sometimes
even their own.

In winter, evergreen pines shame
naked hardwoods stripped of plumage, now
become the decaying blanket above which naturally
nervous sprinters scamper across claw-scarred
branches, ever vigilant for

the huntsman whose cannon shatters worlds
and depopulates the playground. The pines
are silent and wise. They see everything,
tell nothing, and they do not scream

when lightning scars their hearts or whiskery old
men with chainsaws drop them down to earth.

        The creek is an artery
        threading through the scented woodland
        the spongy straw and leaves
        part in deference to its dark course.

Below the paddling mallards, scaly bass
glide, along with perch, bream, and even gar
unannoyed by summer's viperous moccasins
and snapping turtles, that rest now in hidden
hollows only the brave dare plunder.
They pack along the muddy bottom, the sandy

base of the shallow abyss, constantly foraging,
forever fidgety because all fish
are fidgety, even when there are no reptiles
to make life more challenging. Reptiles eat fish, you know.

It's cold at the bottom,
colder at the top—
fish are content to spend their days deep
down. Clever fishermen will find them, though,
if it's their day to find and the fishes' day to be found.

A visitor to the winter woods is stricken
by the silence, scratched only by the squirrels' paws
scurrying over bark and the squirrels bark, too,
like limb-bound pups, untraceable to carpet-bound
intruders quite unnerved by the stillness, unless
of course they're seasoned and journeyed here for that
very reason, in which case, they're not

intruders at all but children to whom
        solitude is a prized possession
        not a toy but a favorite book
        a comfortable escape
from warm fires the uncles gather around,
smoke and make noise, or football on TV with its
ridiculousness and noise, or the out-of-staters in
for Thanksgiving with their troublesome boys who'd rather

tear the house apart than walk in the woods on a brisk
afternoon.

Most astute are swivel-necked owls, perched
in the shadowed crooks where no squirrel plays—
owls are serious business.

They scan for mice, who aren't half as smart
as squirrels and think themselves secure in the damp
red oak leaves. The owls are particularly fond
of rodents unfamiliar with recognized retreat
routes. These are sweet appetizers, much easier
to obtain than the squirrels that bite back and thrash

and often leave bunches of feathers at the scene of the attack.
But owls too are savage, so it really doesn't matter.

Seroquel in the morning slides me on
down before coffee to ground's-eye view
with a rosy-edged hue, foggy like
the dream I just woke from. I like it with
country music so I can hear the words

and feel the pain. Pain keeps me alive,
aware of where I am, but I can challenge
it with a little white pill—too much
pain is deadly—switching out the light
while keeping its heat, that glaring reminder, on
my face. Funny how, when all that's left
are memories, the past is chewed down to its
DNA and even the centipedes' footfalls
          crash like thunder.

When everything ahead is gone, we step back
and suck the marrow from time-dried adventures.

There are panthers in the woods back home,
bobcats that spring upon the owls that spring
upon the mice that nibble broken acorns
dropped by squirrels that pause long enough
to ascertain they aren't endangered, and the fish
hug bottom as dark water gurgles
along to someone else's woods, someone
else's fears, retreat, safe haven
          or hell.

Winter is for greedy sinners rich
in carnal lust, but even in the woodland's
heart, a sinner's greed is just a part
of nature, the do-or-die berater, and every
creature has its time to do and die.

What will the winter thaw uncover? Will we
find lodged in icy sheaths a prehistoric
remnant, a long-forgotten sojourner lost
to the season's sacramental impatience? Perhaps

the mystery of a vanished fighter who missed the bloody
war yet, arguably, survived squadrons
who lived to tell their tales to the grave? Ain't none
of that in Toro Bottom, by the way.

Give us a clue to your killer's face when the snow
peels back in spring. Give our forensic shamans
the account of your stolen youth so we can put
down the beast real slow—and maybe
when the worst is over, the thing revealed

will be ourselves, our pathetic sins attesting
that regardless our assessment, we're far colder
                than frozen death.

It's a cyclic affair, the rolling of the seasons,
overseen by pines and squirrels and children
seeking silence amid the subtle violence
of a world of bones and trails leading nowhere.

Count

Count time—
        everyone on your bed
        face forward
        no talking
        laughing
        singing
        no friends
        family
        joy
        hope.
Count clear—
free to go
        nowhere
free to be not free
until next
count time.

Stats

Angola: 6200 poor, doomed sonsofbitches
Embraced by razor wire-topped fences,
Tunica Hills labyrinth, slate-faced
Mississippi River, and 18000 cursed acres.

90 percent won't get out alive,
you know, 'cause Louisiana's a death state:
kill 'em 'til they drop of old age,
then plant 'em at Point Lookout for safekeeping.

Winter

Winter brought its sinners, losers,
god and godless choosers.
We rolled back the clock
while the clock kept ticking,
lived in fragments, figments,
forgot our reasons
and pretended.

Brother rolled his eyes,
said, "The family's crumbling."
He didn't buy his wife
a Christmas card,
went out and killed an animal
then sighed away the truth.
A machine answers his phone
so he can be alone.

Sister beds her stud
under his mother's roof;
the old woman listens,
blushes, whispers,
"Slut" and smiles at breakfast.
Sister doesn't call.
Sister doesn't write.
Says she's homesick for
the flatlands.

Mother's in the mountains,
cloud dweller high
where trivia doesn't blow,
only snow.
She drifts in the wind
to ancient places;
her children's faces
glisten in snowflakes
that fall to earth
and melt.
She doesn't know what to do
so doesn't.

Eighty-two:
seventeen winters
Gram's lived alone but
never more alone

than she can remember.

She doesn't remember much
these days, just
those she doesn't like,
not why,
and nobody can take that.
She lives in a haze
once home,
withers and forgets.

Beacon

When in the depths of my perplexity
I flounder in tides of self-pity
and in every spiteful surge search
for sounder reasons to exist
despite the pall of varied eccentric sins—

when from rejected amends
I hurl my voice
through a secret solemn night,
petition the darkness
to stay my breath;

when I resolve I have nothing
of honor in my name
and would prefer a gruesome death,
I think of you
and all my despair is reconfirmed.
Bitch.

Traveler

I've seen the world and claimed its treasures,
drank of many distant charms and frightful
pleasures; scraped my knees in Arab sands,
fingers raw from clawed mysteries
uncovered one grain at a time. The African sun
thrashed me at Thebes, robbed my sight at
Khartoum and I loved every elegance of the past.
I saw Ozymandias; I saw Tut's tomb;
I climbed the highest steppe and flashed the moon
while waltzing in the shadow of greats,
who by their immortality earned the title.
I've see the world, and it looked so familiar.

In the gardens, the ghosts of scorched Pompeii
slandered my whispered fascination in
bedroom porn in the Casa dei Vettii
potent enough still to cast a blush.
Vesuvius smirked godlike behind us,
reminded us how insignificant our
feeble constructions, our fragile bones—
   and the table was set for two
   but the lights went out and no one
   thought a lot about dinner after that.
We lounged in the forum at Pompeii's heart,
strolled the via Stabia where wealth
once thrived, mourned in Apollo's temple
victims who rustle through forever;
how curious that we've been here before.

On the heights, great city above the clouds,
we sat in the grass, lazy in the sun
where Spaniards couldn't train their vulture eyes.
You were as lovely as an Inca princess.
The mountain sang with your throaty laughter.
We swayed by the alter where priests invoked
gods we've long forgotten but who look on
their proud city's husk and must wonder how
the damned whites discovered their kingdom's crown.
I wept in the corner of a thousand
lamentations, wept when the world grew gray
and every creation turned to dust—

   I've seen you in places you've never been.
   I've seen the world from a barred womb.

A pacifist tool

It's a pacifist tool, the Christian peace
designed to put our minds at ease and
convince us all that
       God is present
              in the deepest trench,
                         in the driest desert:
all we have to do to be saved
is as we're told—mighty bold
from a pagan's point of view.

Dark date

A proffered date,
prim, paradoxical engagement–
unashamed, I asked her over.

I tumbled down.
She arrived when I needed love,
while I nursed my misery and
a bottle of blues reserved for the special occasion.

How exciting, enlightening,
our private evening!
Her practiced routine–
this gentle angel cloaked
in glossy promise so tender–
embraced my anxiety;
not even the nosey neighbors
suspected we were lovers.

We danced through a dream fog,
a velvety black swirl,
to bittersweet orchestrations,
that soft, solemn dirge.
She held my hand, took my pain,
and I understood,
the sudden clarity exquisite,
beautiful.

They found me and drove her away.
They think I'll forget her.
I still have her number.

Dismembered silence

There is no sun in any place;
this house is death.
I do not tremble.
I am violent.
I am lost.

There is no sun in any place;
I have looked upon the faceless sky
and seen dismembered silence.
Love is no longer possible, nor life;
I am empty.

I have not slept, and I have dreamed.
I have not believed in my heart
in glorious surprises,
in hopes and desperations,
and the anguished hour
with hands outstretched
does not change.

Nightfall in the lonely bed,
emptiness shining in the windows;
I awaken at midnight
and nothing has changed.
Time runs down me like fingernails.
I am alone.
Defeated and ignored, I die obscurely—
now more than ever I understand:
there is no sun in any place.

Dragging on

Just keep dragging on
        old & tired
        used up, expired
& running on fumes,
taking up space,
going going going nowhere—
shoulda got there
a coupla decades ago.
But on I go.
So tired.

Ah, the cruel way—
        slowly self-destructing &
no one knows.
Here in my room with
shades drawn, lights out,
darkness is my dearest friend,
the frightening things that stir in my shadows
my only company.

Vanity alienates me.
I'm repulsed by peers, but
their absence scores
what's left of my humanity.
  Again I consider the cruel way
  and those who chose that embrace—
talented, misunderstood, decomposing
in their own genius.

Oh so lonely in my room but
preferable to the yapping of fools.

Uninvited

A moon as gray as weathered slate
adorns her gleaming neck with sheens
of shadowed silver; here between
the mist of lust and sleep a fate
has crept in through the garden gate
uninvited, unseen.

She sleeps the sleep a castled queen
would sleep among her chiefs of state,
dreaming of some tranquil place
alone beneath a madman's stare—
her breath, her lips, her sculpted face,
her secrets soon I'll claim a share.

And when the morning fills her eyes,
she'll find the light a woeful glare.

*Prison rodeo: guts and glory

He stood panting,
sweat-soaked.
Filthy in the heat of
an April sun,
he watched the beast
watch him.
Focus on him,
snarl, drool, hate
on him,
the antagonist
under 20,000 eyes,
cacophonic roar for
either to outwit the other—
gladiators, man
& beast, prisoners each
and neither
walking away with
a damned thing.

*Previously published in *Exiled Voices, Portals of Discovery* (Nagelsen, 2008)

Dark fall

It comes again, stealthy, assured,
ancient claws scraping across the ceiling,
the walls, the floor,
the quintessential old friend
encroaching from the corner where it waits,
always waits, watching as I stumble over some subtle
trigger, some diminutive trauma
enhanced by self-imposed isolation's paranoia.

Paralyzing, the dark, and heavy enough
to crush a soul. We trade places—
where I was the shadow shimmers,
and my husk cowers in the corner,
unwilling onlooker to a wasted life.
But I lack the resolve to disappear,
so that's something.

So hard to think, to move, to breathe;
its gray fangs pierce me,
darkness enfolds me, and I sink
into that hopeless well, thick water,
suffocating, not caring.
My silhouette peering from above,
musing, whatever is happening, so what?

It's a slow descent.
I've never found the bottom.
Each time I reach down and tug myself
toward the sun, somehow.
I wrestle through suffocating tendrils.
I think, I move, I breathe once more
life into that withered husk,
and the dark retreats to the corner
from where it watches, and waits,
for the next crisis.

PART II

Six haiku

Through a screened window
  blackbird perched in razor wire
my dreams fly away.

September heat wave
  Louisiana jail cell
torment, sweat and tears.

Men in white jumpsuits
  hoe ditches in endless fields
while thinking of home.

Bathing in my sink
  the shower's hours away
I smell like a skunk.

It's just as lovely
  sunset over prison
as sunset at sea.

No smokes, no money
  nothing but the habit left
to rail my weakness.

Bugs

They come when I'm not looking,
the tiny little bugs,
and creep inside my tattered brain
like syrup-slurping slugs.

I often think I'm going mad
each time the slug-bugs crawl.
If only I were small like them
I'd roast and eat them all.

The greatest blessings

In my seemingly often imperiled life
I've had occasion to petition my god,
usually upon having made the sobering discovery
that I'd been thrust headfirst (and by my own folly)
into a precarious corner and as a last resort,
when failure seemed imminent and I was satisfied
that no living being on the face of the earth
could curtail the certain impending disaster,
to lift my wretched person from the proverbial
tumultuous seas of human despair,
or grant me that single, sudden, life-changing
problem-vanquishing request, or simply
rain down upon me good fortune
for a change, and though many of these
cries found favor, I must confess in this moment,
this sentimental moment of unblinded reflection,
the greatest blessings came when I wasn't looking.

II

I've traveled far in this crazy world,
this baffling, confusing menagerie called life;
followed the footsteps of pious and scoffer,
the pathways of both the fool and sage,
content to proclaim myself a crusader
on a fearless mission to uncover truth
or something like it; stumbling, staggering,
questioning, quizzing, refusing to conform
or accept the apparent fruits of my journeys,
sometimes begging of my fellow man
a mere morsel of wisdom to tide me
over the abyss of the vast unknown,
sometimes longing for a wall or a tree
to lean against when I perceived I could go
no farther (the world is full of crutches,
which I've often sought and seized,
but crutches can be caskets, I've learned), yet
in the silence of a clear understanding, I offer
to report that the greatest blessings came
when I wasn't looking.

III

From my youth they taught me that God knows
our every need and will provide and protect
and lead the way to ultimate bliss,
but in my simpleton grasp I found
that God's interpretation of bliss
and mine were quite the opposite, so what
can a man resolve than to set off afoot
into the strange, stern wilderness, into
the incomprehensible desert, to struggle
as best he knows to find the answer
to the riddle, the divine declaration that all
occurs for a purpose (what purpose?),
but like a rowboat adrift in menacing waves
that may never reach the safety of the shore,
or at best in shambles, I tossed and turned
with no direction, frequently blinded
on a drunken carousel of self-defeat;
thus, no answers were found and only now,
my own efforts thwarted, can I admit that
the greatest blessings came when I wasn't looking.

IV

I suppose I lost my self-confidence (if ever I had any)
somewhere along the way.
Perhaps it fled as indestructible
institutions collapsed into dust around me
time and time again; perhaps
I was simply born to flounder awhile
and in my bewilderment sought someone to follow,
some mortal monument of manhood
after whom to pattern my dispositions,
but it never occurred to me that we are all
bestowed with individuality and almost always
to attempt to live the life of another
results in compassionless personal cataclysm.
I crawled from one lion's den to the next,
praying steadfastly when the beasts collected
at my throat, cursing fate, cursing life,
dying faster and faster each day,
and I never realized that the greatest blessings
came when I wasn't looking.

V

Now I'm older, somewhat wiser,
having learned from failure, having discovered
that truth was never so elusive as I persisted to envision.
Truth inhabited my heart all along,
even spoke to me with a whispering voice
some describe as conscience, others, the voice of God;
all I had to do was slow down long enough to listen.
I've known the dark side of life, and I've known
the light, this latter brimming with love
and wisdom, firm direction, that special
blessing granted those who follow
the voice within, the soft, gentle
voice guiding those who will hear,
and in those moments past when I listened came
my blessings, unpetitioned, unexpected,
the simplistic joys overlooked, miracles unmasked
and even undeserved but nonetheless bestowed:
yes, the greatest blessings came
when I wasn't looking.

Ways

My love—
crystalline streams,
unhurried grace,
whispers of billowed dreams
glittering, glowing, the surreal source
of echoes of
southern breezes,
springtime's perfume,
an ocean's hypnotic melody,
the triumph of dawn,
golden flames,
devouring uncertainty,
the spirit unbound, untamed—
a world just for you.

A dark rose

In this great liquid silence
abandoned by men
    a beast lives
who expects nothing from the world.

In this silent garden
    she comes in the night hours,
    in the night of being;
the beast warms her blood.

She remembers a winter's shadows,
sitting where ancient paths lead;
    the glances of a man,
    a dark rose, crushed by time—
the dream floats,
naked and laughing.
The beast warms her blood.

Post-election

So they went and elected themselves a leader.
Most gritted their teeth and voted for the woman.
The ones who mattered gritted and chose the man.
So the man became The Man.

The winners rejoiced. The losers cried.
Universities offered counseling and chaos credit.
High schoolers skipped classes.
Nobodies demanded recounts.

Then wild herds of modern-day hippies with nothing
else to do took to the streets. Some wore masks,
some hoisted profane posters, some postured for the press.
They stomped and shouted and fought the cops,

cursed The Man even though they didn't know him
or what he stood for (but maybe I'll see myself on CNN!).
Not my president, they cried, burned a few flags,
smashed a few windows for good measure.

What are you protesting? the reporter asked.
We're protesting The Man. He's a racist, homophobic,
misogynistic xenophobe. He's an elitist, warmongering
Nazi. He doesn't pay taxes. He's white.

Did you vote? No, I protested.
Did you bleed for that flag?
No, I'm a pacifist.
Ever live in a country without cops?
I wish.
Got a job? Yes! I'm a protester.

And there you have it. Democracy in action.

All the while The Man built his machine.
It's how it goes. Like it, leave it, or stuff it.

They turn on a four-year cycle. Winner and losers.
Nostalgic old-timers say once there was dignity in loss,
grace, respect, and acceptance. Bullshit. Nobody
wants to be a loser. Nobody respects a loser.

It's all in how you define the term.

The wait

It's like dying,
the wait:
uncertain
afraid
unable to forestall the
inevitable
unknown direction.
  Unfair.
Business in order,
instructions passed,
the world is tight
except
the wait tears
at the threads of
patience
logic
birthing extreme images
always adverse
always looming
threatening the
security of complacency.
Shadow of fate, the wait.

Remembering Karla

Congrats on killing Karla Faye Tucker,
you big-eared, monkey-faced motherfucker.
She did everything she could possibly do
to prove to the world and prove to you
   she'd changed, she wasn't deranged,
   she managed in prison to rearrange
her life, she gave it to God, she wanted to live
in Christian fashion, but you let her die.
Hypocritical coward, your life's a lie,
and someday you'll be called on to pay.
I hope the collector is Karla Faye.

Persistent 2005
for Terri Shiavo

They should have let her go years ago.
Vegetation is life long expired,
freaked by being's absence and time's passage:
    a media extravaganza
    for the polemic lonelies.

The family's reason washed out in the spotlight's glare,
spawned truculent ideologies and washtub morality.
They summoned frantic pedantics to champion the cause,
drove legislatures to feeding-tube frenzies,
rebuffed science and vilified her guardian,
whose crime was a promise of death's dignity. They
choked the courts with repeated repetition—frivolity—
and whimpered that she, ages silent, asked not to starve.

She died in 1990. Nurturing her husk is nothing less
than a blight on the face of civility.

Midnight blitz

1.
An echo through a mirrored room,
a teardrop on the floor,
like satin fingers in the night,
implies some secret more.

2.
Take heed to never lift your pride
above the prisoner's state;
just when we think we're not the same
is when we meet his fate.

3.
A second glance at fond romance
would serve the hopeful well;
often what we see as love
is in disguise but hell.

4.
For sleep, for sleep, for sleep I prayed
and prayed until I cried;
God grew weary of my plea
and suddenly I died.

5.
Glory to the wayward mind,
hail the pain-wrought verse;
the poet's life is incomplete
without the poet's curse.

6.
To catch the wind and hold it bound
within a moment's sigh
provides the captor small delight
for caught, the wind will die.

7.
A woman's love, like days of spring,
how brightly shines the sun,
but as a winter's night is born,
her love is swiftly gone.

8.
To live in chains is not to live
but gasp without a breath;
if I were doomed to a tiny room
I'd sooner opt for death.

9.
A pen of gold, a page of silk,
a thought of ivory white;
the poet's finger presses things
that rustle in the night.

10.
A pool of blue the tongue to soothe
when finished is the mile,
is not as sweet when strangers meet
than is a stranger's smile.

11.
He sits to write a verse of love,
he sits unmoved for years;
all the loves that he has lost
induces him to tears.

12.
I prayed to God and asked him why
my life has been so cold.
God said, "Son you are too young.
Ask when you are old."

13.
Thirteen days and thirteen ways
I searched for truth and light;
by the time I found the path
my day had turned to night.

14.
The joy we hold so dear today
tomorrow is a dream
of other times when life was fine;
what does, I pray, it mean?

15.
Midnight holds a certain power
against the gentle mind;
when the clock tolls half-past twelve
our evil deeds we find.

16.
Wipe away the crimson tears,
the blood from off my chest;
the heart is pierced and moaning low,
the prelude to its rest.

17.
Men I've known and women fair,
their names a sullen scatter;
I wonder where they've gotten to,
but then, it doesn't matter.

18.
Take a walk inside my dream,
travel through my mind,
but do not think my restless soul
therein you're apt to find.

19.
In battle should I lose the flag
another would I sew;
a man fights on until the end:
defeat he does not know.

20.
A father to his son is god,
faultless in his ways;
beware then, fathers, in your deeds;
they'll be his someday.

21.
More than ancient wisdom mused
there's nothing mused today;
a limited list, the human gist:
there's nothing new to say.

22.
The deepest hurt is love betrayed,
a wound that never heals;
one should loathe to break a heart
if one knows how it feels.

23.
A branded tongue at day's late end
could be the worse for wear
if when the dawning broke the sky

no more the tongue was there.

24.
Smoke another cigarette,
lose another lung;
before the check has run its course
the bell for you has rung.

25.
Jailer, jailer, with your badge,
lord of men in chains;
remove the badge, remove the chains,
and you are one the same.

26.
Compare the sculpted woman
with one who's blessed to cook;
before the race is finished out,
the cook, I'll book, is took!

27.
Locked into the demon's world
there lies a demon's sea,
from which the monsters of the deep
come nightly after me.

28.
Evil eyes beneath thy brow,
snarling, grinning lip;
behold the mirror of thy soul
whence the reaper sips.

29.
Love is splendid, love is pure,
love is heartless pain;
love is but a double mask
we wear to suit our gain.

30.
Sequined shadows, parasites,
hexagonal stars;
life's a senseless paradox
behind the dragon's bars.

31.
The sweetest lips I ever kissed
I kissed when I was young;

no doubt I would have spit it out
if she had used her tongue!

32.
They say a man will fall insane
if cast out on his own;
I must beg to disagree:
I'm quite at home alone.

33.
The man who cannot share a smile
walks many a long and lonely mile,
rounds many a solitary bend
of barren highways without end.

34.
Tell me, Father, secrets kept
of life's great mysteries;
are you certain that you know,
or are you lost like me?

35.
Mother must you shed your tears
for your wayward son?
Don't you know I'll rise again
when my time is done?

36.
Mother I am not so lost
as fools would have you think;
I've grown accustomed tottering
across the razor's brink.

37.
Blazing, spinning, burning fire
roaring through my brain;
lines and lines of senseless verse
betray a mind insane.

38.
A hundred songs I sent to war,
ninety-nine returned;
thus, of the hundred melodies
all but one were burned.

39.
Cryers in the morning glow
repent of last night's sins,
then conjure up another toll;
the circle never ends.

40.
Ah, the sun, the golden sun
that warms my aged bones
cannot quell my great distaste
for clanging telephones.

Visitor

A witch
a wraith perhaps a night-clad ghoul
watching as I sleep. I
sense her, wake to find her there
shadow-robed near the window.
I'm afraid.
Her face is dark; I can't see her face.
I'm afraid.
At first I think it's Mother,
but this thing is wicked bad.
I'm afraid.
She pricks my toes without moving.
I know she's smiling and
I cry.

I never forgot how close you
stood, my dread that you would take me.
You saw my future trials, grinned
and slipped behind the curtain.

The lovely valley

She was twenty years younger and built like
an architect's dream.
Over the handrail she leaned
to catch a glimpse of
the action below,
and when she bent, I
bent too and pretended to look low
but looked instead down
her blouse and reveled
in the valley.

Pagan

Every time it thundered,
darkness burned.
Sleet slammed against my face and
made me laugh.
When stars were turned and
truth became the coveted prize of
coveters' common race,
I sat and smoked before I
blew away.

Once I climbed mountains.
Those were ignorant cliffs
with bare summits
and barer souls.
The preachers' echoes, doomsday
sayers, gave me pagan vertigo
and an upset stomach.
I don't climb mountains anymore.

In the woods,
in the gray watching woods
I built an alter
to the secret sins of society's
sinless saints,
lopped the head off a longneck
and dumped its bubbly blood
into my greedy pit
to see if I could dance naked with
darkness without being
struck down.
I could.

The neighbors called the cops.
I called a taxi.
The cops are slugs and
I'm a puff of smoke.

Twenty years later

Here I sit twenty years later
        (on the same stool, puffy-eyed, pooch-bellied
        backwoods gator,
        the same saloon and brackish brew, bloated buffoon
        surrounded by the same lonely souls,
        their victimized accounts routinely told
        with slurred exaggeration, self-exoneration
        unnecessary but part of the game—
        it's not about the whys and lies
        but sweet release between the thighs
        forgotten in the next drowning moment)
thinking myself the noblest bastard in the joint.

We poets

We poets,
if I may be so bold to include myself
among the ranks of this noble breed,
are curiously lonely folks
who often exude an air of sadness I suspect
is the creed and code of
creative minds; interaction
strains the bounds of normal satisfaction
because we're not normal.
The chain reaction produces,
destroys, in parallel refraction of
stable versus just plain strange—
it's most unsettling to me as
a man alone with verses, stanzas, scribblings,
when I'd rather arrange a meaningful merger
with a redhead's eager bones—
women and poetry pound like a bass in my head.
I just wish I had more of one than the other in bed.

About the Poet

JOHN CORLEY is a recipient of a PEN America award for playwriting and a National Council on Crime and Delinquency PASS Award for journalism. His work has appeared in recent textbook editions of *Criminal Justice in Louisiana* and *The Wall Is Strong; Corrections in Louisiana*, the literary anthology *Exiled Voices: Portals of Discovery*, *The Angolite*, *BleakHouse Review*, *The Toastmaster*, and other publications. *Pagan* is his first poetry collection.

About the Artists & Designers

CASEY CHIAPPETTA is pursuing an MS in Justice and Public Policy at American University. She recently graduated summa cum laude with a BA in sociology and received the Outstanding Scholarship at the Undergraduate Level. Her research interests include work conditionality clauses and insecure work, urban ecology, and the effects of legal aid on low- and low-middle income individuals. Chiappetta is the Chief Operating Officer of BleakHouse Publishing. In this role, she is responsible for all matters relating to the daily operation of the press and website management.

SONIA TABRIZ graduated from American University (2010) *summa cum laude* with University Honors and a B.A. in Law & Society and Psychology. She received the Outstanding Scholarship at the Undergraduate Level award for her award-winning works of fiction, legal commentaries, artwork, presentations, university-wide accolades, and academic achievement. Tabriz went on to attend The George Washington University Law School, where she served as a Writing Fellow and Editor-in-Chief of a law journal. She is now an attorney in the Washington, DC office of a national law firm. Tabriz is the Managing Editor of BleakHouse Publishing and designs the text for various publications.

CARLY THAW is an illustrator, photographer, and designer originally from Charleston, West Virginia. She graduated from American University in 2018 with a BA in Graphic Design. She is currently working as a graphic designer for Bailey and Glasser, LLP and she continues to do freelance and contracted graphic design work for local performers and artists.

Other Titles from BleakHouse Publishing

Silent, We Sit, Emily Dalgo

Black Bone, Alexa Marie Kelly

An Elegy for Old Terrors, Zoé Orfanos

Up the River, Chandra Bozelko

Distant Thunder, Charles Huckelbury

Enclosures: Reflections from the Prison Cell and the Hospital Bed, Shirin Karimi

A Zoo Near You, Robert Johnson et al.

Origami Heart: Poems by a Woman Doing Life, Erin George

Tales from the Purple Penguin, Charles Huckelbury

Burnt Offerings, Robert Johnson

www.ingramcontent.com/pod-product-compliance
Lightning Source LLC
Chambersburg PA
CBHW051037030426

42336CB00015B/2914